W9-CHE-558

Usborne
Planet Earth
Mazes

Illustrated by
The Boy Fitz Hammond, Susanna Rumiz,
Valeria Danilova, Rachael Saunders
and Lucy Semple

Designed by Claire Thomas

Written by Sam Smith

The mazes at the beginning of the
book are easier and they get more
challenging as you go through.
You'll find solutions to all of
them on pages 61-64.

Rhino rescue

This sanctuary rescues orphaned rhinos so that one day they can return to the wild. Which way should Ruth go to feed all the rhinos at the white signs, then help load the rhino who's ready to be released onto the truck? (She doesn't want to have to double back.)

RHINO RESCUE

FINISH

When rhinos are ready and in good health, they are released back into the wild.

Human contact is limited so the rhinos don't become too dependent and lose their natural instincts.

Ruth

White signs look like this.

Rhinos are fed milk, leafy plants, fruit, vegetables and hay.

If a rhino isn't well, it is sedated so the handler can safely examine it.

Salty seas

Some seas on Earth contain so much salt that people can sit in them and the water will support their weight. Megan's come to this seaside resort for a natural spa experience – guide her through the shallows, between the rocks and bathers, to join Mary, trying out the mud bath along the way.

Megan

Mary

MUD
BATH

Redwood return

The redwood trees of California can live for thousands of years, and are the tallest trees on the planet. Can you lead Chad the chipmunk back to his burrow at the base of one towering trunk?

FINISH

Chad

Cub competition

Earth's North Pole is almost constantly covered by shifting sea ice. Which is the shortest way for the baby polar bears to reunite with their mother – walking over the ice, or swimming in the sea?

Mother bear

Baby polar bears

Cycling in the city

Over half of the world's people live alongside millions of others in busy, built-up cities. Can you help Sam cycle across town to meet his friends at The Shake Place, avoiding any traffic or construction work?

Sam

LIBRARY

THE SHAKE PLACE

Thermal throngs

Hot springs are frequently found near volcanoes, and bathers seek them out to wallow in their warm waters. Help Harriet find a path to the empty pool so that she can enjoy a relaxing hot soak by herself.

FINISH

Harriet

8

Kangaroo catch-up

Australia's deserts, grasslands and forests are full of creatures that are unlike those on any of Earth's other continents. Can you guide Cory along a clear route between the rocks and bushes to catch up with his kangaroo friend?

Cory

Cory's friend

Rice in the rain

Billions of people on the planet mainly eat rice, and the farmers in Asia rely on heavy monsoon rains for good conditions to plant their crop. Find Rishaan a route on the grass between these flooded fields so he can collect some more rice plants from the storage hut.

Rishaan

Storage hut

High-tide hurry

Bill and Toby have been exploring the cave at the end of the beach but now the tide is coming in quickly. Pick out a clear path for them to hurry back across the sand to reach the coastal trail.

Bill and Toby

SEAGULL BAY

FINISH

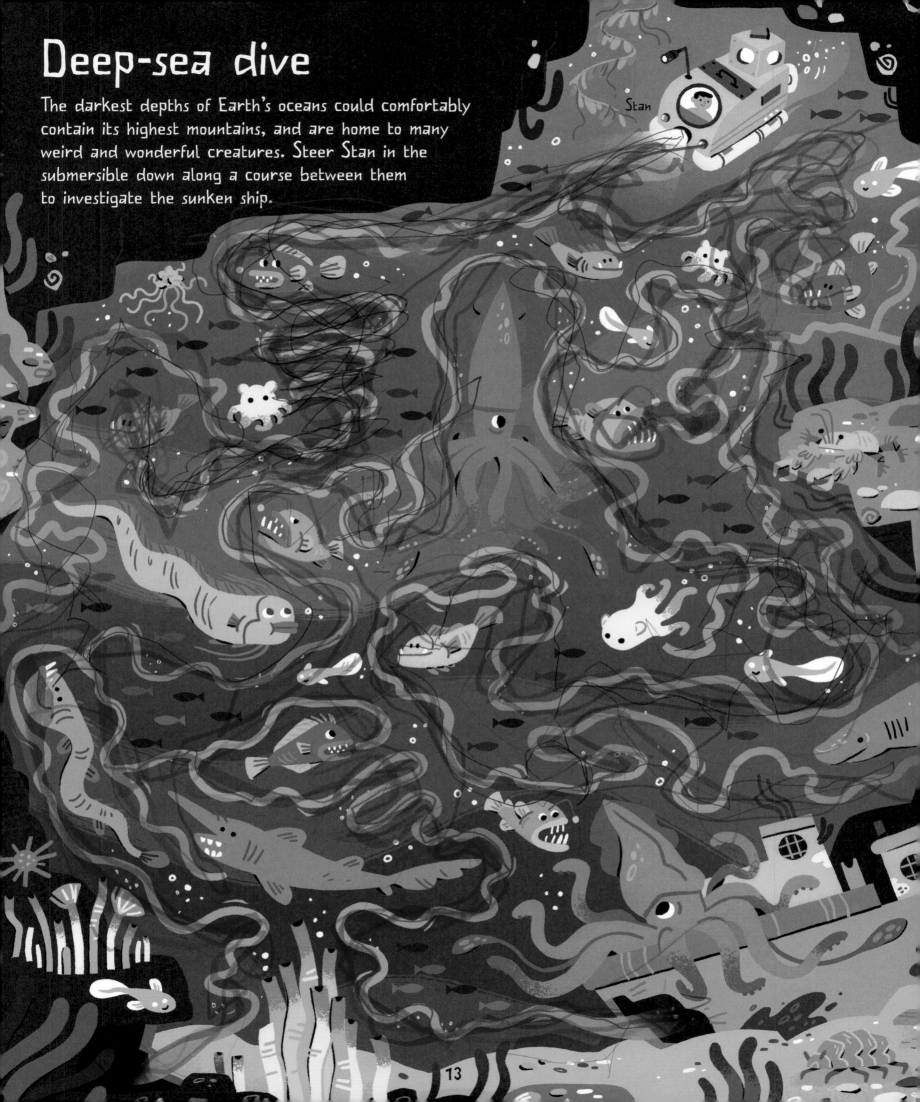

Deep-sea dive

The darkest depths of Earth's oceans could comfortably contain its highest mountains, and are home to many weird and wonderful creatures. Steer Stan in the submersible down along a course between them to investigate the sunken ship.

Stan

Digging for dinosaurs

Scientists study the buried bones of extinct animals, preserved in fossil form, to learn about prehistoric life on Earth. Nate needs help near the head of this newly discovered dinosaur – can you find Roy a route through the dig site to reach him?

Roy

Settled snow

Extreme conditions are common in some places, and people have to be prepared so daily life can continue. Find a route for the snow truck to clear every road in this town and return to the depot without going anywhere twice.

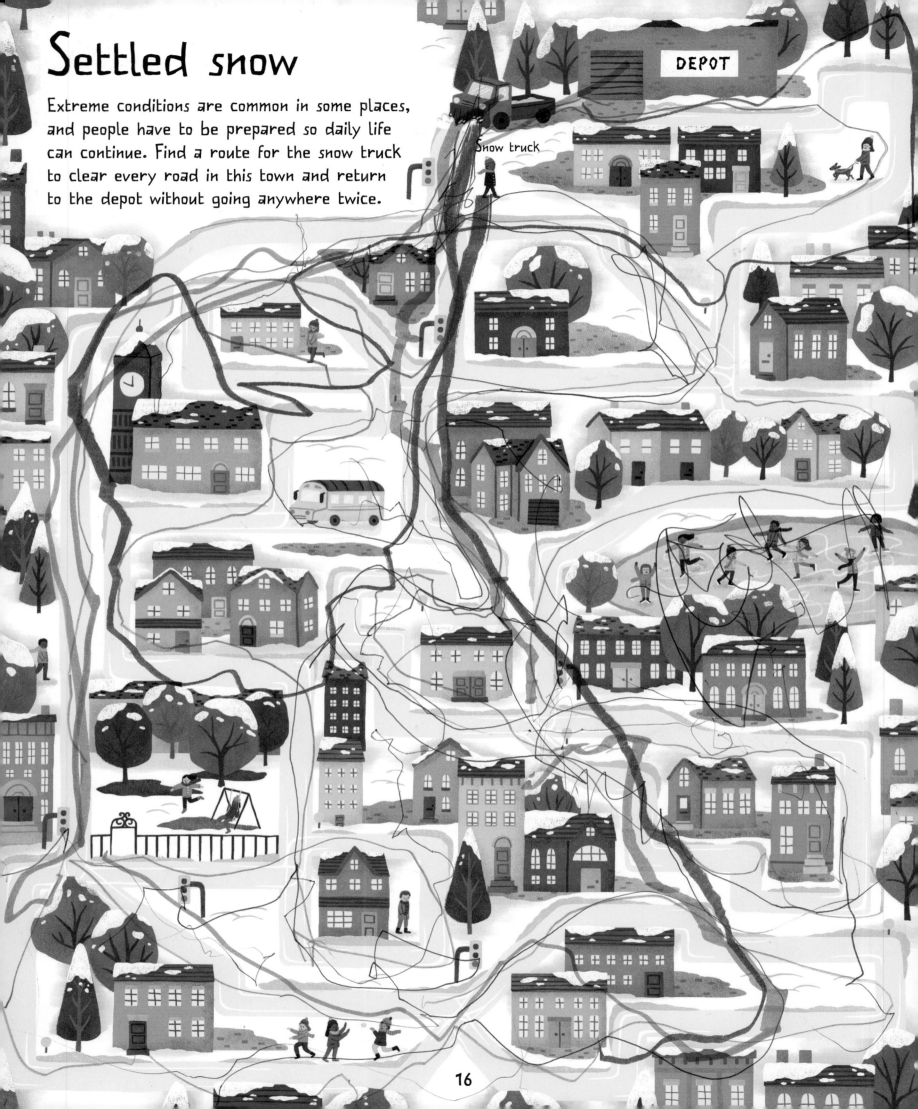

DEPOT

Snow truck

Tornado trouble

Strong whirlwinds called tornadoes can sometimes sweep along the ground under storm clouds, tearing up whatever lies in their way. One tornado is currently on a course close to this town – can you guide Trevor's truck back to his shelter in case he needs to take cover?

Trevor

Trevor's tornado shelter

Swim through the swamp

The Florida Everglades provide unique conditions for plants and animals, and are home to a wide range of wildlife. How can Cody the American coot swim along these swampy waters to his friends without passing any lurking alligators?

Cody

Cody's friends

Lightning landing

Inside storm clouds, ice crystals collide and create huge electrical charges that are then released as thunder and lightning. This helicopter must land immediately – direct it down between the clouds to the helipad, so it doesn't fly through any lightning forks or heavy rain.

Gushing geysers

When water runs over hot, volcanic rocks deep under the ground, it boils and bursts up through natural vents to make spectacular sprays of steam. Pick out a route over the rocky terrain so Sara and Greg can go and watch this geyser erupting.

Sara and Greg

FINISH

Running rivers

Under the sun's warmth, seawater evaporates and rises into the air. High in the sky, it cools into clouds and then finally falls as rain or snow, forming rivers that return to the sea. Which way will this rainwater flow from the highest lake here as it heads along the rivers, over the waterfall and back down to the open ocean?

START

FINISH

Mining minerals

Miners dig deep into the Earth to find fuels, metals and minerals under the ground. Guide the dump truck through the middle of this mine to pick up some ore from the purple excavator and take it to the processing plant, avoiding the rock piles and any other vehicles along the way.

Dump truck

Ore

FINISH

PROCESSING PLANT

Coral conservation

Coral reefs sustain all sorts of sea life, but can't survive when the water gets too warm. Find Ruby the researcher a route to study all the dying white coral and return to the boat without swimming anywhere twice.

Ruby

Grand Canyon guide

Over millions of years, the Colorado River has carved its course through many layers of rock, creating this vast canyon in America. Guide Grace through this stretch of it, using the stepping stones to cross the water, so she can rest at the Weary Walker Café.

Grace

WEARY WALKER CAFÉ

27

Polar research

Scientists have set up research stations at the South Pole so they can monitor things like wildlife, the weather, and the melting of the ice. Steer Bonnie's snowmobile along a path between the penguins and polar experiments to help her team launch the weather balloon.

Bonnie

Big drills bore down deep into the ice to see what's beneath and find out about Antarctica's history.

Wildlife is weighed and studied to check the health of some species' populations.

Weather balloons are sent high into the atmosphere to measure wind speed and pressure.

Scientists record and document animals to understand and learn about the ways they behave.

29

Flash flooding

Heavy rain has made the local river burst its banks, leaving large parts of this town waterlogged. Find a flood-free route from the school for Fiona to pick up her brothers from the park and hurry home to their house with the blue front door.

SCHOOL

Fiona

Fiona's brothers

Slow descent

Rainforests are home to more animals and plants than any other habitat on Earth. Which way can Suri the sloth climb down the tree trunks to the water, avoiding the patches of slippery moss, so she can go for a swim?

Suri

Distant destination

Lucy's long-haul flight has just landed and she's hopped on the airport bus – can you find it a route along the roads to Stormwood Station, then take the train so Lucy can be picked up from Tolbrook Terminus?

Stormwood Station

Airport bus

TOLBROOK TERMINUS

Satellite signals

Communications companies use satellites in space to beam data to places all over the planet. Can you pick out the path that this signal will take from the transmitter to the receiver so that it only bounces off six satellites?

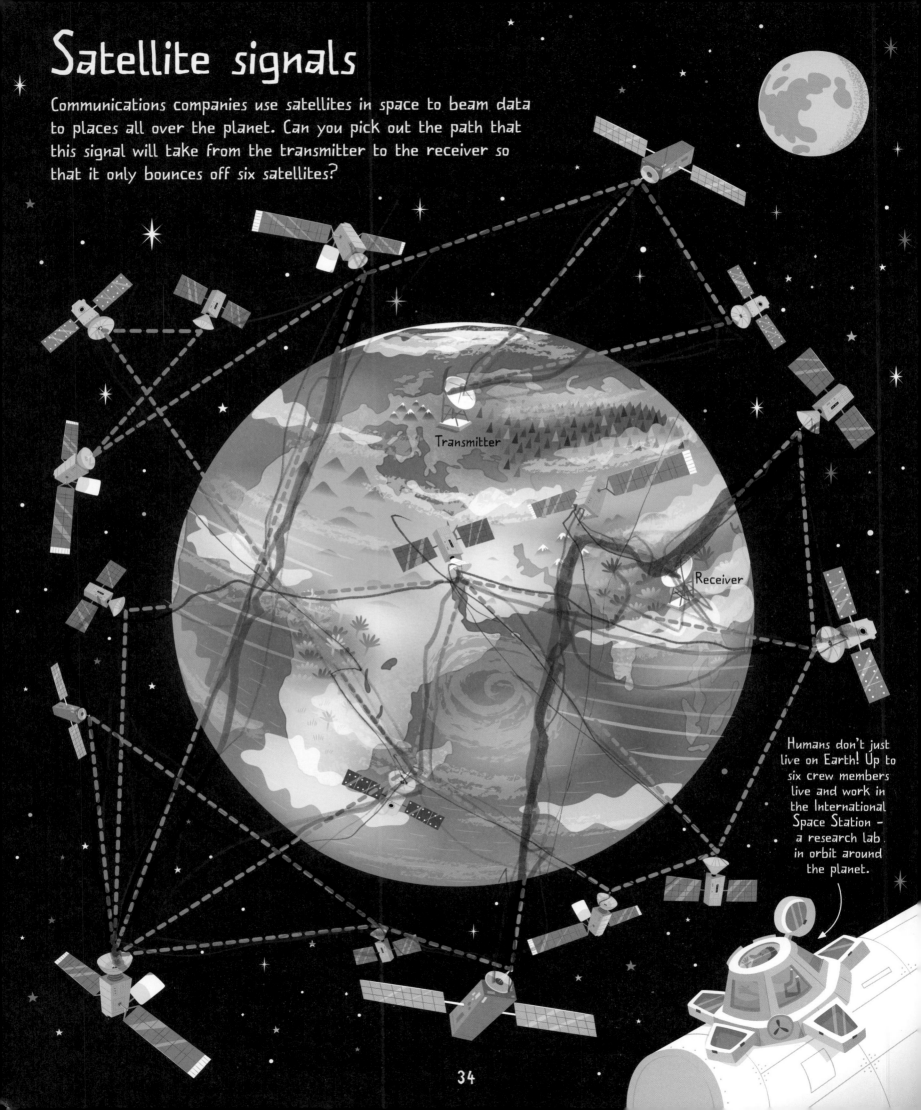

Transmitter

Receiver

Humans don't just live on Earth! Up to six crew members live and work in the International Space Station – a research lab in orbit around the planet.

Northern Lights

High above the North Pole, tiny particles blown out from the sun hit Earth's atmosphere and create spectacular light shows in the night sky. Help Ned navigate the Norwegian roads so he can watch the Northern Lights from the observatory. (He can pass other cars on his way.)

Observatory

Ned

Recycling sort-out

To protect the planet and avoid running out of resources, people must recycle waste materials to use them again. Follow the arrows on the sorting belts in this recycling plant to show the route that plastics take to the bailer.

START

HAZARDOUS WASTE

CARDBOARD SORTER

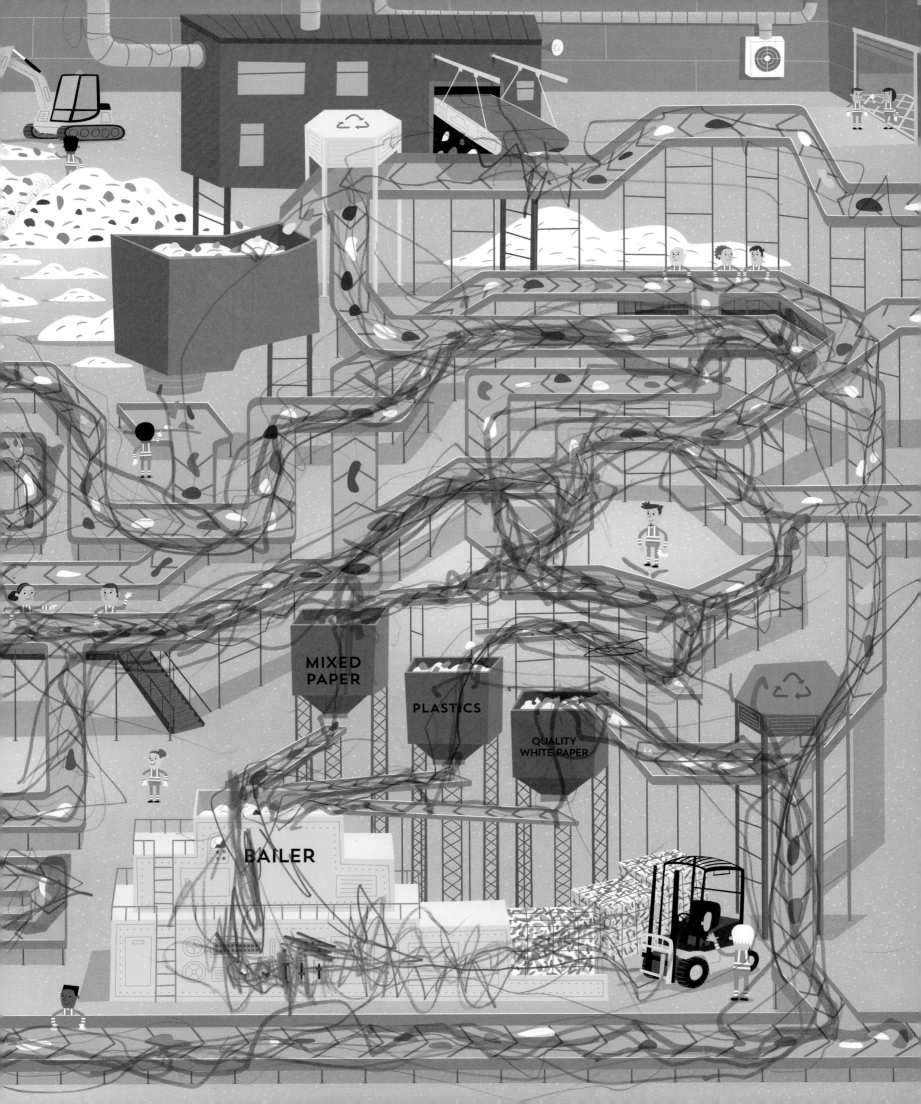

Unexpected eruption

A team of geologists has been studying volcanic activity on this island, but the latest eruption has started earlier than anticipated. Steer their vehicle along a clear route away from the volcano, crossing any bridges they need to, so they can reach the rescue boat and escape.

Rescue boat

Geologists

Magnificent Madagascar

Madagascar is home to all sorts of amazing wildlife that cannot be found anywhere else in the world. Plan a route around the island, starting at Antsiranana, so you can see each animal marked on the map and finish in the capital, Antananarivo, without going anywhere twice.

Antsiranana

Chameleon

Tomato frog

Madagascan flying fox

Bamboo lemur

Antananarivo

Fossa

Mouse lemur

Leaf-tailed gecko

Ring-tailed lemur

Red fody

Comet moth

Underground grottos

Over thousands of years, rivers and rainwater slowly wear away softer rocks, carving out caverns deep underground. Help Crystal use the ropes and bridges to navigate this network of caves so she can study the sleeping bats.

Crystal

FINISH

Majestic mountains

Earth's mighty mountain ranges rise up into snowcapped peaks that climbers seek to conquer and skiers love to speed down. Can you help Lars and Frieda carry their skis through these foothills so they can take the cable car up to the alpine cabin?

FINISH

Lars and Frieda

43

Power-line problem

Networks of cables carry electricity across large distances to power people's homes. The unlit houses here have lost power – follow the cables back to see which substations have faults, then lead the engineer to both, and back to the main plant, without taking any road twice.

FINISH

Engineer

SUBSTATION

SUBSTATION

SUBSTATION

SUBSTATION

SUBSTATION

SUBSTATION

POWER PLANT

Migration map

Many animals move in huge herds to new locations to survive the changing seasons on Earth. Lead the herd of wildebeest along a safe route to the watering hole, so that they avoid all the lions and leopards lying in wait along the way.

Lion   Leopard

Watering hole

Wildebeest herd

Environmental energy

The local energy inspector wants to clean up Coaltown so that it runs on renewable energy instead. Find him a route to the town, so he can visit all the marked areas of interest and assess the options on his way, without taking the same road twice.

Energy inspector

Biofuel power plant

Hydroelectric dam

Solar panels

Tidal lagoon

Coaltown

Wind turbines

Solar farm

Geothermal power station

Renewable energy sources

Biofuel power plants generate energy by breaking down natural materials, such as the oils in plants.

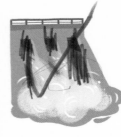

Geothermal power stations use volcanic forces in the Earth to produce energy.

Hydroelectric dams trap a vast volume of water, then release it all at once to turn huge turbines that generate electricity.

Solar farms use arrays of thousands of solar panels to convert heat from the sun into useful energy.

Solar panels can be attached to the roofs of individual houses to power people's homes.

Tidal lagoons produce energy by using the natural movement of the tide to push seawater through their turbines.

Wind turbines tower above the ground, using high winds to generate electricity.

Protecting the planet

An Australian film crew is touring the globe to find footage for a new documentary called 'Ways To Protect Our Planet'. Plan a route for them so they can visit each point of interest and return home without going anywhere twice.

ORGANIC FARMING

Some farmers avoid pesticides, and find ways to protect crops that are less harmful to the environment.

ELECTRIC VEHICLES

Manufacturers are now producing cars that run on cleaner fuels to reduce levels of pollution.

REFORESTATION

People plant more trees to try to preserve Earth's rainforests and revive rare habitats.

RECYCLING
State-of-the-art machines sort through thrown-away materials so we can reuse resources and reduce waste.

POLAR RESEARCH
Scientists monitor the melting of Earth's ice caps, and look for ways to stop rising ocean temperatures.

REVIVING RIVERS
Volunteers help to clean up polluted rivers to protect wildlife from harmful waste.

OCEAN CLEAN-UP
Engineers have developed devices to try to catch and remove plastics from the ocean.

ANIMAL CONSERVATION
Special reserves protect endangered animals and release them back into the wild.

Film crew

49

Estuary exploration

All kinds of creatures can be found living along estuaries, where the mouths of rivers meet the sea. Which way should the wildlife watchers go to see every marked animal in this estuary and return to Tidetown without revisiting any part of their route?

Wildlife watchers

Tidetown

Gulls

Egrets

Lapwings

Dragonflies

Dolphins

River otters

Seals

Salmon

Ducks

50

Primate pictures

Mountain gorillas make their homes high in the forested foothills of tropical Africa. Guide the primatologists past every gorilla here to get close-up photographs and return to their shelters without retracing their steps.

Primatologists

Arid adventure

Deserts are the driest places on the planet, but some people still find ways to survive in them. Help Coman complete his long trek across the scorching sand to the oasis, herding up all his camels along the way. He must avoid snakes and scorpions, and doesn't want to retrace his steps.

Coman

FINISH

Forests of the future

Large areas of forest are cut down for fuel, construction and farming, so to sustain habitats people must plant more trees in their place. Pick out a path so Sri can put a new tree in all the flagged positions and return to where he began, without doubling back or re-entering any dug-up plot.

People cut down trees for fuel, timber or to make paper.

Sri

Trees are a vital part of the environment, and are home to many amazing animals.

New trees need to be planted to replace those that have been cut down. This is called reforestation.

French forecast

The weather forecast has predicted these conditions over France. Map out a route for Carly so she can drive to Montpellier in her convertible, avoiding all the storms, heavy rain and strong winds.

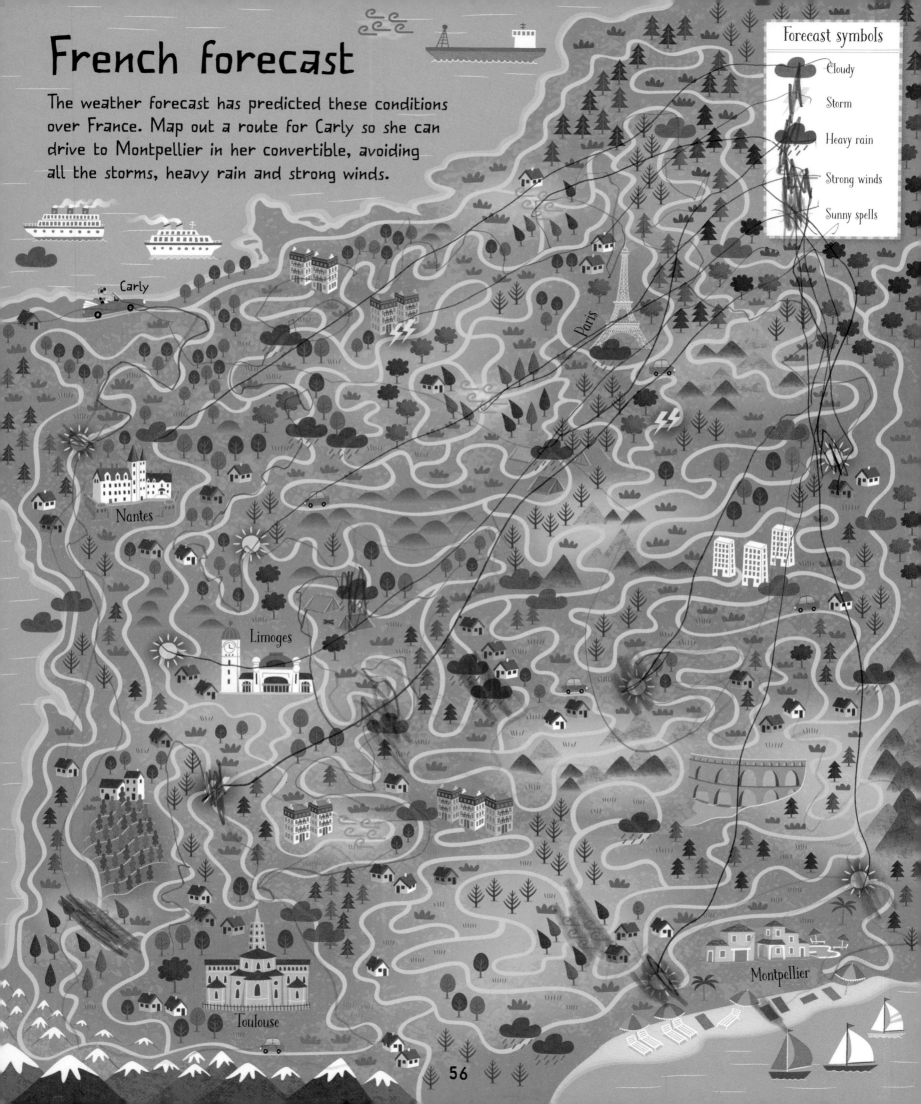

Forecast symbols

Cloudy

Storm

Heavy rain

Strong winds

Sunny spells

Carly

Paris

Nantes

Limoges

Toulouse

Montpellier

Dolphin detour

Dolphins live in social groups called pods, whose members are in constant communication with each other. Can you lead Dusky between these islands to round up the rest of the dolphins and then rejoin the pod, without doubling back?

Dusky

The pod

Farming for food

Farmers cultivate large areas of the countryside, planting crops so people have enough food. Can you help Freddie pick up produce from all the marked fields and deliver it all to the market without going the same way twice?

Produce to be picked up

Farmers' market

Freddie

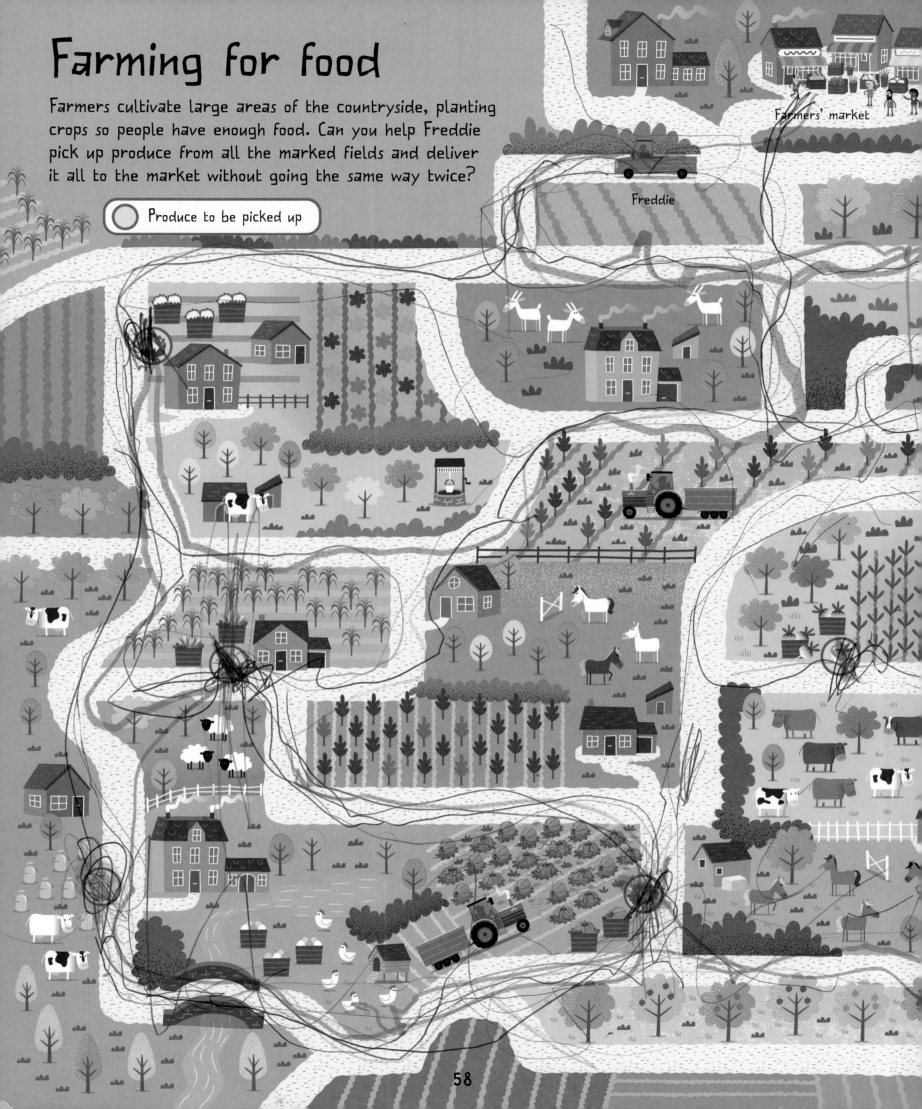

Plastic pick-up

These volunteers are clearing litter from the river to protect wildlife and prevent the plastic from reaching the sea. Bella is bagging up the purple bottles – help her collect them all and take them to the sorting team on the bank without retracing her steps.

Bella

FINISH

2-3. Rhino rescue

4. Salty seas

5. Redwood return

6. Cub competition

7. Cycling in the city

Swimming is the shortest way.

8. Thermal throngs

9. Kangaroo catch-up

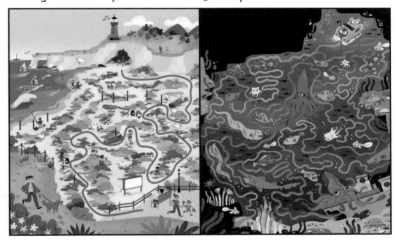

10-11. Rice in the rain

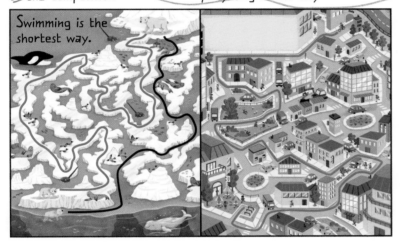

12. High-tide hurry

13. Deep-sea dive

14-15. Digging for dinosaurs

16. Settled snow

17. Tornado trouble

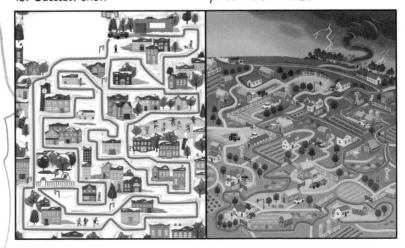

18-19. Swim through the swamp

20. Lightning landing   21. Gushing geysers

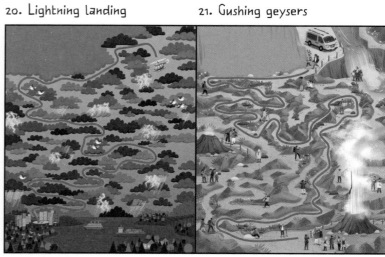

22-23. Running rivers

24. Mining minerals   25. Coral conservation

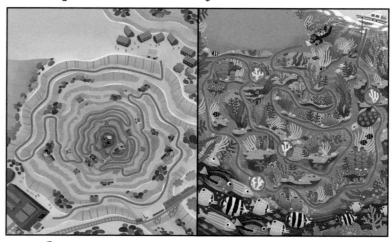

26-27. Grand Canyon guide

28-29. Polar research

30. Flash flooding   31. Slow descent

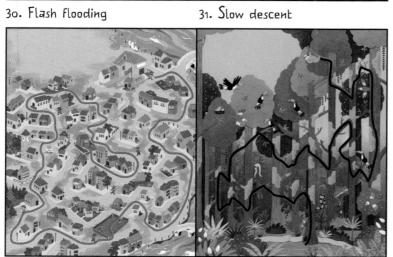

32-33. Distant destination

34. Satellite signals

35. Northern Lights

36-37. Recycling sort-out

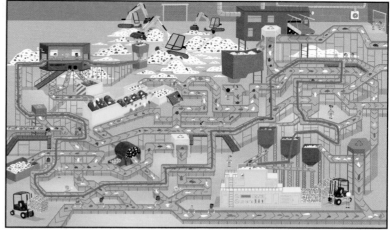

38-39. Unexpected eruption

40. Magnificent Madagascar

41. Underground grottos

42-43. Majestic mountains

44. Power-line problem

45. Migration map

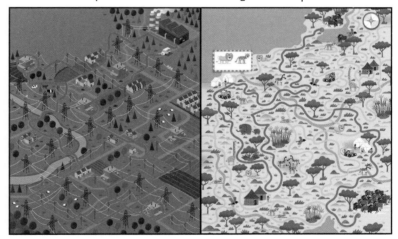

46-47. Environmental energy

48-49. Protecting the planet

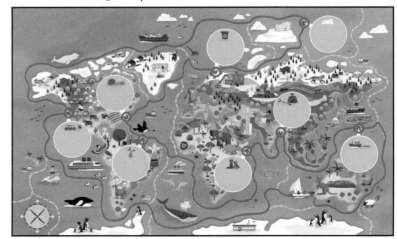

SOLUTIONS

50. Estuary exploration

51. Primate pictures
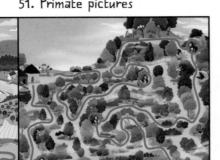

52-53. Arid adventure

54-55. Forests of the future

56. French forecast

57. Dolphin detour
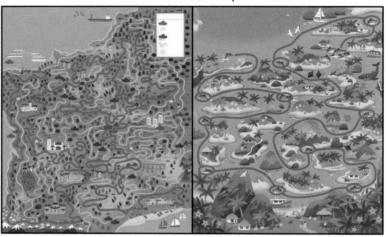

58-59. Farming for food
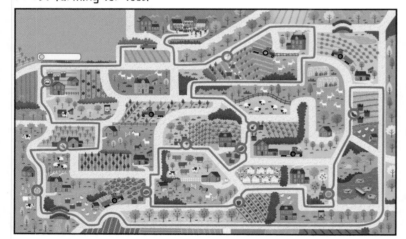

60. Plastic pick-up

Acknowledgements

Cover design by Candice Whatmore

Edited by Sam Taplin

First published in 2020 by Usborne Publishing Ltd., Usborne House, 83-85 Saffron Hill, London EC1N 8RT, England, usborne.com
Copyright © 2020 Usborne Publishing Ltd. The name Usborne and the devices 🎈🌐 are Trade Marks of Usborne Publishing Ltd.
All rights reserved. No part of this publication may be reproduced, stored in a retrieval system, or transmitted in any form or by any
means, electronic, mechanical, photocopying, recording or otherwise without the prior permission of Usborne Publishing Ltd.
First published in America in 2020, UE, EDC, Tulsa, Oklahoma 74146 usbornebooksandmore.com Printed in China.